30-MINUTE SOLUTIONS SERIES

How to Hold Successful Meetings

30 Action Tips for Managing Effective Meetings

By

Paul R. Timm, Ph.D.

CAREER PRESS
3 Tice Road
P.O. Box 687
Franklin Lakes, NJ 07417
1-800-CAREER-1
201-848-0310 (NJ and outside U.S.)
FAX: 201-848-1727

30-MINUTE SOLUTIONS SERIES:
HOW TO HOLD SUCCESSFUL MEETINGS
Cover design by L & B Desktop Publishing & Printing

Printed in the U.S.A. by Book-mart Press

To order this title, please call toll-free 1-800-CAREER-1 (NJ and Canada: 201-848-0310) to order using VISA or MasterCard, or for further information on books from Career Press.

Library of Congress Cataloging-in-Publication Data

Timm, Paul R.
    How to hold successful meetings : 30 action tips for managing
effective meetings / by Paul R. Timm.
        p.   cm. -- (The 30-minute training series)
    Originally published: [S.1.] : Jack Wilson & Associates, 1994.
    Includes index.
    ISBN 1-56414-325-2
    1. Business meetings.   I. Title. II. Series.
HF5734.5.T55   1997
658.4'56--dc21   97-7917
                                                           CIP

Contents

Foreword

Been to Any Good Meetings Lately?

To some people, asking if they've been to any good meetings lately is like asking if they've had any pleasant dental surgery.

The frustration of those who have for too long suffered unproductive business meetings shows up in statements like: "A meeting brings together a group of the unfit, appointed by the unwilling, to do the unnecessary," or "When all was said and done, a lot was said but nothing was done."

A lot of organizations hold too many meetings and, to compound the problem, the meetings are inefficient *and* ineffective.

Why is it that many meetings lead to feelings of restlessness, disgruntlement, and raw boredom? Do meetings have to be such a burden? What can be done to make meetings live up to their potential to produce high-quality results?

Good questions. I'll show you some answers that can make a radical difference in the ways you do business. The trick is in applying Action Tips that will insure productive and even enjoyable meetings.

✎📁 **Chapter 1** ✎📁

The Need for Better Meeting Managers

The problem of ineffective meetings is widespread and increasing. Here are a few facts.

Fact: A survey conducted by a business-communications consulting firm revealed that more than 70 percent of executives consider many of the meetings they attend to be a waste of time. Despite this, 67 percent of the respondents report that they had to attend more meetings this year than the year before. (*Success* magazine.).

Fact: According to Frank Snell, author of *How to Win the Meeting*, executives spend more than 75 percent of their work time in meetings. That's a lot of time!

Fact: Studies suggest that as people rise to executive-level positions, the time spent in meetings increases. An advertising letter for Xerox Learning Systems reports that the senior executive "will devote nearly five hours of *every* working day to leading and attending meetings. This is a conservative evaluation." Later in the same letter, it is noted that "executives now spend 100 percent more time [in] meetings than they did just 10 years ago."

Fact: Meeting overkill is a significant contribution to job stress. Yet our thinking about the nature of work is shifting. Work is being seen as a source of more than just income. Nothing meaningful is accomplished if people aren't enjoying the process. In short, when work is fun, people produce more and better output.

A key term here is "fun." Just what, exactly, is fun? For most people true fun is equated with productivity and satisfaction. It's fun and it feels good to accomplish something. It's fun to know that we have power to achieve team success. It's fun to grow as a person and develop new skills and abilities. It's fun to know that we are increasing in value every day through our experience and learning.

That may be a somewhat different definition of "fun" than you're used to, but think about it: Aren't these the kinds of things that really give you lasting good feelings? If your job is overburdened with nonproductive meetings, you are probably not having much fun. Indeed, the current thinking in management theory suggests that productivity, that is, the employee's perception that he or she is accomplishing something useful, actually produces job satisfaction rather than the other way around (that satisfaction causes people to be more productive).

Better meeting management is particularly fertile ground for having some fun on the job. And the good news is: *You* really can have control over the frequency and effectiveness of your meetings. Mastering new skills—such as the ones I'll show you in this program—can create a tremendous sense of satisfaction. And your job will be more fun!

But you don't have to take my word for it. You can try it for yourself. In fact, I challenge you to make a commitment today to try the skills and ideas in this program for 30 days and see if you don't have more fun on the job. What have you got to lose? Sign on the dotted line below and let's see what happens.

I, _____ hereby commit to trying these meeting management Action Tips for 30 days to see if I will actually have more fun on my job. In doing so, I will sincerely try to apply each of the techniques presented in this program. If nothing gets better, I will go back to the old ways of doing things and forfeit all the potential fun I could be having.

Signed _____ Date _____

"Meetings, of course, do serve a purpose. Consider this: Our national economy is based on a 35- to 45-hour work week. Without meetings, this figure would dwindle to a few hours at the most. Our whole system, as we know it, would collapse."

—Stephen Baker, *I Hate Meetings*

Okay, we have that whining out of our system. Cynicism aside, I have a better idea for dealing with the need to have meetings: Let's get better at the process so that meetings will become more productive and satisfying to participants. In so doing, we will boost the effectiveness of any organization.

Are meetings frustrating but necessary?

Meetings are often frustrating and sometimes not necessary. Many people get highly frustrated by the frequency and quality of their organization's meetings. At the same time, the value of employee participation in decisions, an idea that found support in early human relations studies of the 1940s and 50s, continues to be accepted as a truism.

Indeed, best-selling management books consistently reinforce the need for open, fluid, informal, and frequent participation by employees of all levels in organizational problem-solving. That seems to mean a full and perhaps increasing use of meetings, albeit perhaps less formal ones.

The evidence seems to conclude that: 1) meeting attendance is an often unpleasant, unproductive, or frustrating experience for participants and leaders; 2) the use of decision-making meetings is potentially useful, although perhaps overused in some organizations; 3) meeting use is generally increasing; and 4) many people lack skills necessary to be effective as leaders or participants in the "group process."

This book is your action guide

In the rest of this book you will find:

1. A series of Action Tips—not just vague philosophies or general musings about the topic, but implementable tactics that will allow you to make all your meetings successful.

2. A number of pencil and paper activities and self-evaluations to get you thinking about meeting effectiveness.

3. Guidelines for evaluating and improving your meeting management skills.

Please write in the book freely, jotting down ideas that may be triggered—especially ideas you can apply immediately to improve the ways you use the awesome potential of the group process.

How do *you* feel about the meetings you attend?

Take a moment to complete the brief questionnaire on pages 12 and 13. This survey seeks your reactions to problem-solving meetings held in your work organization.

Beside each statement, please circle whether you strongly agree (SA), agree (A), neither agree nor disagree (N), disagree (D), or strongly disagree (SD).

Respond to each item in terms of your experience at work. Your experiences are likely to be different in social, recreational, or religious organizations, so please focus on job-related meetings.

The meetings I attend at work

1. Result in high-quality decisions.	SA A N (D) SD
2. Take up more time than they are worth.	SA (A) N D SD
3. Result in participants' feeling good about the group's decisions.	SA A N D (SD)
4. Seldom result in creative solutions or ideas.	SA (A) N D SD
5. Often fail to reach a sense of completion.	SA (A) N D SD
6. Seem to be substitutes for more meaningful work.	SA A (N) D SD
7. Produce better solutions than could be produced by one person working alone.	SA A N D (SD)
8. Usually result in decisions that could be more quickly made by one person working alone.	SA (A) N D SD
9. Promote a commitment toward the organization by involving members in decisions.	SA A N (D) SD

10. Permit group members to freely participate and share ideas openly.	SA (A) N D SD
11. Move through the discussion phases efficiently.	SA A N D (SD)
12. Are called only when necessary.	SA A N D (SD)
13. Begin and end on time.	SA A N D (SD)
14. Deal with agenda items that are not relevant to all participants in the group.	(SA) A N D SD
15. Allow offbeat or unusual ideas to be given a fair hearing.	SA (A) N D SD
16. Follow an agenda rather than wandering to different topics.	SA A N D (SD)
17. Are scheduled too frequently.	SA A (N) D SD
18. Are often dominated by a few members.	(SA) A N D SD
19. Cause participants to gain a feeling of organizational unity.	SA A N D (SD)
20. Seem to eat up too much of my workday.	SA (A) N D SD

How do your scores compare with other folks? Compare your responses against those summarized in Appendix 1.

As I suggest specific ways to make the most of your meetings, I'll focus on Action Tips that overcome the typical pitfalls—the problems that most often detract from meeting effectiveness. See if you recognize some serious problems in the following case of Moose Lips Corporation.

Moose Lips Corporation: a case in point

Here's a little story to set the stage for our discussion. See if you've ever experienced anything like this:

∽ ∽ ∽ ∽

The president of Moose Lips Corporation meant well, but somehow things just didn't work out quite the way he thought they would. Matt Bayless had built Moose Lips from a one-man operation working out of his garage to the largest manufacturer of camping and recreational gear in the Pacific Northwest.

Despite rapid financial growth, Matt had the uneasy feeling that things wouldn't continue to be so good. He was disturbed by a marked rise in production costs and an apparent increase in competitor activity. Nothing specific, but he was just uncomfortable.

Then he hit on an idea.

After dusting off a management textbook he'd read in college, Matt decided to use "participative decision-making" to cope with the company's problems. "Sure, that's it," he decided. "We'll have a big meeting and get some new ideas."

His memo to all employees went out the next morning. Everyone was "invited" to participate in an all-day retreat at the Homestead Resort and Conference Center about 20 miles out of town. The agenda was set. The employees would all be getting together to "share their ideas" on how to retain market share, how to cut production costs, and "any other topics relevant to the success of their business." The entire company would be shut down all day Friday while the 126 employees conferred.

A few days before the big meeting, word filtered back to Matt that a number of the Moose Lips employees had been grumbling about having to spend a whole day at the Homestead.

They already were feeling a lot of pressure to keep up with their work, and, in fact, they were coming up on the busiest time of the year for several departments. Besides, no one seemed to understand what was supposed to be accomplished at the proposed meeting.

Matt was upset by the grumbling. After all, participative decision-making was supposed to make workers feel good. Everything he read said PDM is the way to go. So he sent another memo to answer their objections. He explained in a tone that didn't succeed at concealing his irritation that, while no specific proposals were expected to be voted on at the meeting, he felt that the opportunity to "share input" was very important, and he expected everyone to be there.

The big day came, and 115 people showed up for the all-day retreat. In the opening session, the president said that he was concerned about market share and production costs. He then indicated that, to be systematic, the morning would be spent in 12-member "buzz groups" dealing with market share. Each group would report back to the larger assembly just before lunch. The afternoon would follow a similar schedule but would deal with production problems.

The buzz groups were assigned randomly, and everyone, including Matt and the other company officers, participated. By 5 p.m. when the meetings broke up, it was clear that most participants were frustrated by the futility of the whole process. Employee grumbling had become a dull roar. No one, including Matt, could clearly describe what had been accomplished. And the net cost to the company went far beyond the charges for the rental of the facilities and the catered coffee breaks and lunch. The costs included well over a thousand work hours.

∽ ∽ ∽ ∽

What went wrong? Take a moment to write down the problems. Where did Bayless goof?

We'll refer back to Bayless and Moose Lips Corporation later in this book. But first, let me ask a few questions: Is this case all that unusual? Do fiascoes like this happen often in business? Are managers generally making the most of their meetings?

If you or people you work with are falling short of their true potential in the use of meetings and group problem solving, read on. The Action Tips presented in the rest of this book will go a long way toward overcoming the kinds of pitfalls experienced by Moose Lips Corporation, not to mention the troubles you and your business are likely to encounter without strong meeting skills.

Chapter 2

When to Hold a Meeting (and When Not To!)

∼ Action Tip 1 ∼

Don't overuse meetings.

Far too many of us in the business world hold a meeting every week—say, Tuesday at 10 a.m.—simply because we've always held a regular meeting at a regular time. Meetings become an organizational cliché. We meet out of habit instead of out of necessity. Sometimes we aren't even sure what advantages or disadvantages are associated with using this communication medium, the meeting. Try the brief activity that follows.

Advantages and disadvantages of meetings

Before we can make rational decisions about the use of meetings, we should consider the inherent advantages and disadvantages of the group decision-making process. In your own words, what are these?

Five potential advantages of meetings:

1. _____
2. _____
3. _____
4. _____
5. _____

Five potential disadvantages of meetings:

1. _____
2. _____
3. _____
4. _____
5. _____

If you had trouble articulating advantages or disadvantages (perhaps you simply haven't given them much thought), you run a serious danger of overusing meetings.

Following are some possible responses, although the words you use to describe advantages and disadvantages may differ. The point is that meetings should not be held without thinking about the pluses and minuses of the process.

Frequently mentioned advantages of meetings include:

1. Getting diverse opinions or ideas.
2. Providing opportunities for participation.
3. Identifying actions and assigning responsibilities or delegating tasks to employees.
4. Sharing important information or updating groups on business activity.
5. Inspiring and motivating attendees.
6. Increasing opportunities for employee interaction and networking.
7. Getting to know co-workers better.

And the disadvantages? Meetings are often considered:

1. Time-wasters.
2. Costly.
3. Lacking of coherence or progress.
4. A way to avoid making difficult decisions.
5. A way to deflect individual responsibility.
6. A discouragement to creativity.
7. A stress-inducer to already overworked employees.

◡ Action Tip 2 ◡

Never let meetings become a substitute for action.

Some managers use meetings as an alternative to making the tough decisions. Consciously or unconsciously they hope that by "talking it out" they can avoid the unpleasant necessity of acting. For some, it's hard to face up to the fact that filibusters are seldom a useful management technique.

Ultimately a successful meeting must reach some decision—either a solution to a problem or a decision to take other action. If it doesn't, it's likely to be because the problems or issues haven't been clearly defined, the participants aren't really motivated to reach a solution, or some procedural roadblocks haven't been handled well.

The best way to overcome the problem of meetings as substitutes for action is to *demand action* from the meeting. In other words, insist that some conclusion be reached. Have a pretty good idea of what can realistically be expected from a group. Let the group know what is expected. Be a manager, not just a moderator.

◡ Action Tip 3 ◡

Count the cost.

Meetings can cost a lot of money. A group decision inevitably takes more time than an executive action. And the costs of such time can really add up. Example:

Meeting cost:

Estimated salary of meeting participants	
(@ $30,000 year) = hourly	$ 15
Number of participants	x 12
Hourly meeting cost	$180

A four-hour meeting can easily cost $720 in direct labor costs alone. And this figure doesn't include the added "burden" costs for each employee—benefits, Social Security, medical coverage, etc. Typical companies add at least 25 percent for such benefit costs.

Count the cost

How much are meetings costing in your organization or department?

First, figure the approximate number of hours you spend in meetings each week:

hours per week: _____

How many people participate (an average figure)?

_____

What is the average labor cost of all participants in the meetings you attend? (Estimate salary plus 25 percent or more to cover benefits.)

Salary (per year)   _____

Benefits   _____

Hourly rate

(divide annual salary by 2,080 hrs./yr) =   _____

x Hours spent =   _____

weekly costs

More difficult to calculate are the psychological costs to the individual and the organization, which can be staggering. Work done by subordinates is often tied up while the boss is in conference. Talented employees engage in monotonous busywork while waiting for direction from the absent leader. Customers are annoyed that they cannot talk with the conferring manager. The manager's work piles up so that he or she is faced with a stack of phone messages to respond to, a pile of papers to sort through, and a half-dozen people who just have to talk about some pressing matter when the conference ends.

All of these situations sap energy from people who are paid to use their minds. And all add to the aggravation of the manager's job.

Overcoming the high costs of meetings

There are two ways of reducing the costs of meetings:

1. Use meetings to deal with problems that can best be solved by groups. Don't use the process as a security blanket. Take the initiative to make individual decisions when you are in the best position to do so and when your decision is not likely to result in opposition.

2. Run meetings efficiently. Later in this book I'll describe a unique way to monitor the costs and effectiveness of your efforts to reach solutions in groups. Learn how to use these tools and use them for more efficient meetings.

The simplest tool we can use to reduce meeting costs and increase efficiency is an agenda. A meeting without an agenda is just a bull session. It may be enjoyable, but little will be accomplished. Try using an agenda planner similar to the one on the next page to identify the meeting's priority, purpose, people, and preparation.

～ Action Tip 4 ～

Make the meeting's purpose absolutely clear.

Meetings are of two general types: informational and problem-solving. Often, information-dissemination can be handled without using a meeting. The most legitimate use of the group process is to bring group perspective on a specific problem, project, or decision.

If your meeting must serve as both an information-sharing and problem-solving session, separate the two in your agenda. Get the informational issues covered first (they usually take less time) and then shift into problem-solving.

Everyone knows why we're here, right?

Wrong! More often than we'd like to admit. Although the person who called the meeting probably has a pretty good idea of why it's been called, others may not.

Agenda planner

Name of meeting: _____ **Date:** _____

Location: _____ **Time:** _____

Priority: What is the urgency of this meeting? _____

_____

_____

_____

_____

Purpose: When we have finished this meeting, we should
have accomplished the following: _____

_____

_____

_____

_____

People: Who will attend? _____

_____

_____

_____

_____

Preparation: What should they bring with them to the
meeting? _____

_____

_____

_____

Even if you think you've conveyed the purpose of your meeting clearly, you might want to try this up front: *Ask everyone in the group to write specifically why the meeting is being held.* Then compare answers. As we try to work down from a general expression of the topic (solving our morale problem, for example) to more concrete objectives (reducing high absenteeism rate among data input operators), we introduce a clearer focus to the meeting.

By clarifying a specific topic up front, you'll know when the task has been accomplished. Then the meeting can end.

∼ **Action Tip 5** ∼

Don't use a meeting when you should act alone.

In some cases, working alone can be more efficient and produce a higher-quality outcome than a meeting. Research has found, for example, that groups have no advantage over individuals when dealing with puzzles or brain-teasers. For some sensitive issues, consulting with individual trusted associates or advisers will produce a better decision than asking for a group decision.

Just keep in mind that the group process is not the answer for every issue.

The following A-C-T distinction helps determine which decision-making approach makes the most sense in a given situation:

A Make the decision alone if:

- The problem is extremely urgent and must be acted upon now.

- The problem involves a "brain teaser" with only one correct answer and you have it.

C Make the decision after consulting individually with others if:

- You lack sufficient information to make a sound decision working alone.

T Make the decision working together with others in a group if:

- The problem is complex and diverse opinions are likely to produce a superior solution.

- You are not choosing among equally adequate options.

- The decision is likely to be controversial, resulting in resistance when implemented.

To further guide your A-C-T decision, answer the following questions. Each yes answer strengthens the case for using input from others, seeking out a consultation or meeting. Each no answer suggests that making the decision *alone* would probably be more effective.

1. Do other people you might involve have sufficient knowledge or experience to make a contribution to the decision-making process?

☐ yes   ☐ no

2. Do they feel some ownership of or concern for the problem such that they wish to help solve it?

☐ yes ☐ no

3. Do they share the objectives and goals of the organization or group who will be deciding upon a solution to the problem? (No counterproductive "hidden agenda?")

☐ yes ☐ no

4. Do they have good communication and interpersonal skills so that they can work together effectively in a group?

☐ yes ☐ no

5. Do they understand the limitations within which the organization must work in dealing with this problem?

☐ yes ☐ no

∽ Action Tip 6 ∽

Try a stand-up meeting.

If the topic for discussion is straightforward and tightly focused, conduct the meeting standing up. People will be less likely to dawdle and drone on.

Examples of when and how this approach might be called for: when the group needs to respond quickly to an urgent situation; when the major purpose of the gathering is to make a simple announcement; or when you meet simply to assign tasks.

In other words, if you don't want extended discussion, don't allow participants to "settle in."

✏️📁 **Chapter 3** ✏️📁

Overcoming Pitfalls in Meeting Preparation

～ Action Tip 7 ～

Invite the right people.

Anyone who is invited to your meeting should meet these criteria:

1. They must have some expertise about the issue or project being discussed. When people in the group don't know enough to deal with the problem (such as all the employees of Moose Lips

Corporation working on productivity issues) the solution will reflect pooled ignorance. The meeting will be unproductive.

2. They must have some involvement or vested interest in the outcome of the discussion. Make sure that departments or people to be affected are represented in the meeting. It becomes extremely difficult to sell a decision—even a good decision—to people who have been denied any input into the decision-making process.

3. They must be reasonably skilled in the group decision-making process. Use people who can express themselves reasonably well and who can appreciate the fact that differences of opinion can be useful. If some participants are known to be inflexible or rigid, take time to create a tolerant climate. Set the tone by saying something like: "I don't expect us all to agree with everything said, but I want to hear all viewpoints. So say what's on your mind and don't criticize other ideas until we can fairly evaluate all input."

4. They should share the overall values of the organization. If participants are antagonistic or in disagreement with the company's goals, it makes no sense to have them participate in decisions affecting those goals.

Be sure, too, to invite the right *number* of people. Have enough to represent a variety of opinions but not so many that the process is bogged down. Ideally, for problem-solving, four to 12 participants works best. Many executives advise that the fewer the participants, the better. I prefer action teams of four or five for most situations.

The Moose Lips case illustrates a pitfall of inviting the wrong people (Matt invited everyone!) and the involvement of groups that are too large. He assigned groups of 12, which were too big to generate a free flow of ideas.

～ Action Tip 8 ～

Assign advance preparation.

The meeting's agenda should not be a mystery. If people are invited to work together, they should know what the meeting is about and what kinds of information and/or ideas they may need to gather and bring with them.

Begin with developing the agenda and distributing it in advance of the meeting. Then, follow up by requesting specific assignments from each attendee. You might assign one individual, for example, to bring and discuss department sales results. Another attendee might be asked to investigate competitor activities. Or challenge all attendees to come to the meeting with three solutions to the problem or issue being discussed.

Assigning preparation succeeds in doing two things: It helps ensure that your meeting will be efficient and effective because you will have all the material and information available then; and it increases attendee contribution and involvement in the meeting.

～ Action Tip 9 ～

Use a written agenda to set expectations.

If the meeting is to deal with a range of issues or concerns, people should have the opportunity to contribute to the agenda.

The following elements should be included in your written agenda:

1. Items to be handled (presented in proper sequence). Be sure to distinguish between *informational items* (where little discussion will be needed) and *discussion items* where participants will be actively involved in problem solving.

2. Start and anticipated ending time.

3. Time for any scheduled breaks.

4. Name of person responsible for leading discussion of issues.

As meeting leader you should have a rough idea of how much time you want to allot for each item. If discussion gets bogged down, use Action Tip 21 to jump-start a stalled meeting.

∿ Action Tip 10 ∿

Avoid producing poor-quality decisions.

While an often-claimed advantage of meetings is "synergy" (the outcome is superior to what could be reached working alone), there are cases where the group process may backfire and negate that potential advantage. Before assembling a meeting, ask three questions. If your answers are yes, you may want to reconsider using the meeting. Here are the questions:

1. Might the group members *lack sufficient expertise* to deal with the problems?

2. Will there be pressures that will *censor the free flow of information* within the group?

3. Is there a likelihood of *conflict* within the group that could become destructive.

I'll show ways to overcome these problems later. For now, consider the possibility that they will occur when deciding if a meeting should be held.

Chapter 4

Overcoming Pitfalls in Setup and Kickoff

∼ Action Tip 11 ∼

Start on time and use a realistic schedule.

A major objection of meeting attendees is the failure to start and end on time. Don't wait "a few minutes until the rest of the folks get here" or you'll find yourself doing so every time. Get a reputation for prompt starts and people will get there on time.

Likewise, don't run overtime. If you've scheduled 90 minutes, stop at or before that deadline. (That'll really shock people—ending a meeting early!) When the work is done, quit.

If you are dealing with a particularly complex issue, schedule several sessions of manageable length, if possible. Tell people you have scheduled an hour just to work on the definition of a certain problem. A second session will articulate decision criteria. Another session will be used to compare possible solutions against these criteria. And so on.

Schedule breaks. Have refreshments. Encourage people to walk around the room. Do whatever is necessary to keep participants energized.

If it appears that the issue will take more time than scheduled, anticipate this before the clock strikes, giving the group enough time to summarize what you've covered, identify what you still have to accomplish, and schedule time for another meeting for reaching a conclusion.

∼ Action Tip 12 ∼

Welcome participants and set the stage.

A simple expression of appreciation to people for coming to your meeting (even if they didn't really have much choice) is a nice way to set the stage for cooperative work. Let people know that they were selected because they can contribute valuable insights and ideas and that you respect their judgment.

∼ Action Tip 13 ∼

Create a positive tone.

By welcoming the attendees and thanking them for participating, you've already taken the first step in setting a positive tone. Keep up the momentum. An appropriate psychological climate is best set by example. Let people know that the discussion can be casual and that they are encouraged to be creative.

Remember, too, that discussion will thrive or die on the communication climate that emerges. Encourage participants to be assertive with their input—but not aggressive. Set the example by eliminating harshly judgmental language or sharp criticism. Remind people that the most useful input is that which is direct, specific, and nonthreatening.

Watch your language cues

Rephrase the following responses so that they will be less likely to act as discussion inhibitors:

1. That idea will never work.

_____

_____

_____

2. You've talked too long already—why don't you let someone else say something.

_____

_____

_____

3. We've tried that before—forget it.

_____

_____

_____

4. Come on, let's stop wasting time and come up with some serious solutions, okay?

_____

_____

_____

5. You get so hung up on the details.

_____

_____

_____

6. The company will never approve of something like that.

_____

_____

_____

～ Action Tip 14 ～

Create a meeting-friendly room setting.

Set up the meeting room so that participants:

• Can see each other face to face (not sit in rows, auditorium-style).

• Are provided with writing materials and a table(s) to write on.

• Will feel free to use a chalk board, flip charts or transparencies to illustrate ideas.

• Are encouraged to move around the room freely to relieve tension or fatigue.

• Are provided with refreshments if the meeting will run more than two hours.

Make sure you have arranged in advance for any equipment, supplies, or materials you will need. Searching for a flip chart or piece of chalk, rounding up more chairs, discovering the VCR doesn't work, or finding out the room doesn't have an outlet where you need it are surefire time-wasters.

Chapter 5

Monitoring and Leading the Meeting

∼ **Action Tip 15** ∼

Be aware of "hidden agenda" items.

Committee meetings seldom have just one goal. There are other, secondary objectives even when the primary task seems clear. Sometimes these "hidden agenda" items, real though they may be, are implied but never stated.

For individual participants they may include such objectives as:

- Getting some "exposure" (to favorably impress others, for example).

- Providing an arena in which we can assert our power or ability.

- Filling some perceived quota for meetings.

- Providing a chance to socialize with others.

- Providing a chance to assert dominance of one group or department over others (or a chance to break that dominance).

- Working on leader and participant communication skills.

- Diffusing decision-making responsibility so that one person won't have to take all the heat if a decision fails.

- Getting away from unpleasant work duties.

When achieving individual hidden agendas doesn't take away from the effectiveness of the group, don't worry about it. If the ulterior motives of the hidden agenda deter the group from accomplishing its work, talk with participants candidly (perhaps in private) and solicit their cooperation in putting the group's needs above their own.

∼ Action Tip 16 ∼

Reward participants' input.

Never let a group member's input go without acknowledgment. To do so will quickly extinguish further input from that person—and others.

Bear in mind that stating an opinion or fact is risky for most people. They risk being perceived as wrong, naive, unimaginative, or any of dozens of other possibilities.

By acknowledging contributions, we create a climate where more will be offered. A simple "good thought," or "you might be on to something there" can draw further input. Even if the suggestion doesn't make much sense, you can come up with a neutral response like "okay" or "thanks." But do say something (unless you want to shut the speaker up).

∼ Action Tip 17 ∼

Monitor pressures to censor.

While you may be encouraging all participants to contribute, you may discover that other forces within the meeting are resulting in a censorship of input. Two common forms of such pressure are:

1. Individual dominance.

2. Groupthink.

In many meetings, certain individuals (or sometimes small subgroups) quickly dominate a discussion. This may be because of their personality, position, or personal status. These people may range from being particularly charming (and thus disproportionately influential because everybody likes them!) to being highly autocratic or stubborn.

The problem is compounded when status differences are involved. A military general working in a small group with enlisted men *will* have more influence—even if he knows less about the topic. Matt Bayless, the president of Moose Lips in the example from Chapter 1, should not have placed himself in one of the buzz groups. He would naturally dominate because he's the boss!

Group leaders need to be sensitive to how differences in status and expertise as well as communication styles can put a damper on free discussion. If you are the boss, back off from interjecting your ideas too soon. Better yet, be quiet, remain neutral, or—if necessary—excuse yourself from the meeting so as not to discourage a free flow of ideas, even ideas people think you might not like!

∼ Action Tip 18 ∼

Recognize and deal with groupthink.

Groupthink describes a condition of like-mindedness that tends to arise in groups that are particularly cohesive. While cohesiveness is normally a desirable condition, it can be carried so far that it becomes counterproductive. This is especially likely when the group has a high *esprit de corps* and where members' desire for consensus or harmony becomes stronger than their desire for the best possible decision.

Under such conditions, critical thinking and the independent and objective analysis of ideas become less important than keeping everyone in the group happy and friendly.

Here are eight symptoms of groupthink:

1. An overemphasis on team play, unanimity, and getting along harmoniously.

2. A "shared stereotype" view that competitors or those in opposition to us are inept, incompetent, and incapable of doing anything to thwart the group's efforts.

3. Self-censorship among group members; personal doubts are suppressed to avoid rocking the group's boat.

4. Rationalization to comfort one another and reduce any doubts regarding the group's agreed-upon plan.

5. Self-appointed "mind-guards" that function to prevent anyone from undermining the group's apparent unanimity and "protect" the group from information that differs from their beliefs.

6. Direct pressure on those who express disagreement.

7. An expression of self-righteousness that leads members to believe their actions are moral or ethical, thus letting them disregard objections to their behavior.

8. A strong faith in the wisdom of their group.

Each of these symptoms of groupthink damages realistic thinking and effective decisions. A combination of several or all of these situations can be devastating to group effectiveness.

Unmasking groupthink

In order to recognize and neutralize groupthink in your meetings, try asking yourself these questions.

* In your own words, why is groupthink a potentially significant problem in meetings management?

* How could groupthink be overcome?

◠ Action Tip 19 ◠

Don't allow conflict to become destructive.

Traditionally, it has been assumed that conflict should be avoided in meetings. The term conjures up images of fist fights or people screaming at each other. In reality, conflict is simply a state of incompatibility, and incompatibility itself is neither good nor bad. What makes that incompatibility either desirable or undesirable is the participants' reaction to it.

We typically respond to conflict in one of several ways:

1. We can attempt to *avoid* conflict by not expressing opposing views and by withholding even nonverbal disagreement. Here we keep from rocking the boat and minimize the possibility of being subjected to rejection or reprisals from others. (Groupthinkers respond this way.) The drawback here is that some good ideas—ideas that can best solve the group's problems—may be withheld.

2. We can engage in unregulated confrontation, which is traditionally characterized by a win/lose orientation, leading to a no-holds-barred, open warfare among participants. The goal here is to win over others at any cost. Unregulated conflict becomes very personal. The result is often the withdrawal of some participants.

3. We can *manage conflict*—the most productive response—by regulating but not eliminating confrontation. Recognizing that the abrasive actions of opposing views—like sandpaper or wood—polish the final product, the skillful leaders seeks free exchange of information but without the win/lose destructiveness of unregulated conflict. Accomplishing this calls for communication skills that encourage the generation of information without inhibiting or turning off participants.

Incidentally, a sense of humor helps. Mark McCormack, author of *What They Don't Teach You at Harvard Business School,* said, "Laughter is the most potent, constructive force for diffusing business tension... Humor is what brings back perspective." Good advice. On several occasions I've seen meeting participants express especially strong views in emotionally charged terms. The stress level in the room peaks—then someone says with a smile, "Gee, Bill, why don't you just say what you're thinking? No need to beat around the bush." The joke diffuses the tension and all participants are able to step back with a more objective perspective.

⌒ Action Tip 20 ⌒

Avoid over-centralized leadership.

Meeting discussions are most effective when there is little intervention from the designated leader. The process of guiding and directing the group's activity is likely to move from person to person within the group rather than being centered on one individual. If each group member takes some leadership role, problems of dominance can often be avoided. The result is what is called "group-centered leadership." This is contrasted with traditional leadership, illustrated in the following chart. (Some of the ideas in this chart were adapted from Leland Bradford, author of *Making Meetings Work: A Guide for Leaders and Group Members.*)

Effective meeting managers work to move the group away from the traditional leader toward group-centered leadership or self-managed teams.

Traditional	Group-centered
1. The leader directs, controls, polices, and leads members to the proper decision. The leader's authority and responsibility are acknowledged by members.	1. The group, or meeting is *owned* by the members, including the leader. All members, with the leader's assistance, contribute to its effectiveness.
2. The leader focuses attention on the task to be accomplished, brings the group back from any wandering, and performs all the functions needed to arrive at the proper decision.	2. The group, with participation from all, is responsible, with occasional help from the leader. The leader is a servant and helper to the group.
3. The leader sets limits and uses rules of order to keep the discussion within strict limits set by the agenda. He or she controls the time spent on each item lest the group wander fruitlessly.	3. All participants take responsibility for task productivity, methods of working, assignments of tasks, and plans for the use of the time available.
4. The leader discourages the expression of feelings or emotions as they are believed to be disruptive to objective, logical thinking.	4. Feelings, emotions, and conflict are recognized by the members and the leader as legitimate factors in the discussion process.
5. The leader suppresses a member's disruptive behavior by talking to the offender away from the group.	5. Any problem in the group must be faced and solved within the group and by the group.
6. Because the need to arrive at a solution or action plan is the goal, needs of individual members are considered less important.	6. With coaching from the leader, members come to realize that the needs, feelings, and goals of all should be met in order to foster team focus.

∿ **Action Tip 21** ∿

Use a systematic decision-making strategy.

Failure to work through a problem in a systematic manner is one of the major causes of inefficient, ineffective, and frustrating meetings.

Most professionals readily understand the process of problem-solving and its importance, yet many seem incapable of or unwilling to apply it in practice. Understanding the decision-making process does little good unless this knowledge is actually put to use.

There are two phases in the development of a decision-making strategy:

1. Problem description.
2. Problem solution.

It's important to describe or define the problem before jumping to the second step. The description phase seeks to crystallize the nature of the problems or issues. Such problems may be attributed to an inability to achieve desired objectives, a dissatisfaction with the speed at which goals are reached, an uncertain sense of morality or ethical standards, or just a general condition of wondering whether the very best is being achieved.

There are three phases of problem description:

1. Definition.
2. Analysis.
3. Reformulation (taking another point of view).

Problem definition

What exactly is causing us to sense that a problem exists? Participants, in the initial stage of discussion, should attempt to identify, in specific terms, the elements of the problem. This process of defining contributing factors usually involves defining critical terms. The group called together to "do something about employee morale" should define what they mean by morale. How do they know whether morale is good or bad?

Often, an operational definition—one that defines in terms of something clearly measurable—works well. In this case, we might say that bad morale is what we have when absenteeism, number of grievances filed, and employee turnover reach some specified level.

Problem analysis

Once the problem is defined, there should be a general discussion of objectives, where we stand in terms of meeting the objectives, and what obstacles we face. The objectives or solution should be described in terms of criteria. For example, we might say an ideal solution to our perceived morale problem would:

- Reduce absenteeism to less than 2 percent per day.

- Reduce grievances filed to one per month.

- Reduce turnover to .5 percent per month.

This defines the objective in measurable terms. We should also develop additional criteria. Criteria statements might finish the sentence: An ideal solution would...

- Not undermine the authority of the supervisor in any way.

- Not cost additional money for wage or benefit incentives.

- Be easily implemented.

- Serve as a prototype for future employee motivation programs.

- Be based on sound management theory.

These criteria should be listed on a chalkboard or chart so that everyone can refer to them as possible solutions are evaluated. Once criteria are established, solution ideas generated in the discussion can be weighed against them.

Problem reformulation: taking another point of view

At times, discussion of the "obvious" problem breaks down and people get frustrated by a seeming inability to come up with workable ideas. If the problem definition and analysis have been carried out and we still have no resolution, the difficulty may lie in our underlying assumptions. The effective problem-solver recognizes that even the best groups sometimes "bark up the wrong tree."

In our earlier example of the employee morale problem resulting in absenteeism, grievances, and turnover, a problem reformulation might be useful. The group's predominant and perhaps unspoken assumption may be that supervisor-subordinate relations are at fault. In reality, some environmental condition such as the presence of harmful chemicals may be the cause of much absenteeism.

Reformulation means taking a new tack, and it can lead to more productive meeting results. Once problem description has been satisfactorily achieved, the solution stage begins. This may involve three more steps:

1. Solution proposals.
2. Solution testing.
3. Action testing.

However, when participants jump to the solution proposals step before the problem description phase is complete, what may emerge could be an excellent solution—but to a different problem!

～ Action Tip 22 ～

Use brainstorming when creative ideas are needed.

The term "brainstorming" has become synonymous with any kind of creative thinking. But that is a misuse the word. Brainstorming is a specific technique using explicit rules for idea-generation and development. This approach requires a communication climate in which free expression of all kinds of ideas is valued and encouraged—no matter how offbeat or bizarre they may seem. Basic rules are:

1. *Don't criticize any ideas.* No comments, no grunts or groans, no thumbs-down gestures. Just let it come out and be recorded.

2. *No idea is too wild.*

3. *Quantity* of ideas generated is important. Push to get as many ideas without regard as to whether they make any sense at this point.

4. Seize opportunities to *hitchhike*—add to or amplify on ideas suggested by others.

The rules of brainstorming are easier to state than to obey—especially the second one. Unless great care is taken, nonverbal cues can be interpreted as evaluations of ideas, which can discourage additional "wild ideas." When using brainstorming, the participants should prominently post the rules as a constant reminder.

The climate that has been set by the meeting leader can promote or hamper the use of brainstorming. A climate that encourages humor and informality will work best.

～ **Action Tip 23** ～

Use a nominal group process when appropriate.

The nominal group process (NGP)[1] is an idea-generating approach that is particularly useful when dealing with potentially emotional or controversial ideas. Rather than having group members immediately speak up with their point of view (a process that may *commit* them

---

[1] This process first came to my attention in *Communication and Group Process, 3rd ed.*, (Holt, Rinehart and Winston, 1977) by Halbert E. Gulley and Dale G. Leathers.

to that view by voicing it publicly), participants write down ideas following a clear definition of the problem or issues. Participants spend 10 to 20 minutes writing out their ideas about possible solutions. Then each participant provides one idea from his or her list, which is written on a flip chart in full view of the group. Ideas are recorded but not discussed at this point.

This round-robin listing of ideas continues until members have no further ideas. Participants may then clarify or amplify on an idea. Then they privately rank the ideas.

The steps of the process, once again, are:

1. Silent generation of solution ideas in writing.

2. Round-robin recording of ideas.

3. Discussion of ideas for clarification.

4. Voting by ranking items (several votes may be needed before a final solution is accepted).

Solution idea evaluation

Once final ideas have been generated, they may be evaluated against the criteria established in the problem description phase. Which ideas, alone or in combination with others, would be most likely to solve the problem?

It is possible that no proposal will meet all criteria fully. You must then predict which is most likely to rectify most of the problems, most of the time.

In other words, in this step the group evaluates its best ideas for solving the problem. This evaluation, of course, is based on the criteria that have been articulated by the group. If the idea seems likely to contribute to solving the problem without negative consequences, implement it and see what happens.

The result of using a careful decision-making strategy, including the three phases of problem description and the three steps of solution generation, should result in better, more productive, more efficient problem-solving meetings. Of course, we can't always successfully predict outcome. Time will be the best test.

∼ **Action Tip 24** ∼

Use a decision grid.

A decision grid provides a way to boil down possible options to a final decision. It is a process that can best be described with an example. Assume that you are making a group decision to purchase chairs. Three steps will be needed to come to this decision:

1. Discuss the decision criteria that should be evaluated. Write these on the "priority matrix" form shown in Figure 1 on page 54.

2. Next, determine the relative importance each of these criteria should be assigned. Write these on the form shown in Figure 2 on page 55.

3. Use the evaluation form shown in Figure 3 on page 55 to make your final decision.

These figures provide examples. Blank copies of the forms are found in Appendix 2.

Figure 1

SIMPLE CONSENSUS PRIORITY MATRIX	A	B	C	D	E	F	G	H	I	J
ISSUE:										
FACTORS:										
A. Sturdy	X	A	C	A	A	F	A	A	A	A
B. Folds to store	X	X	C	D	E	B	B	B	B	J
C. Comfort	X	X	X	C	C	C	C	C	C	C
D. Padded seat & arm	X	X	X	X	D	D	G	H	D	J
E. Guarantee	X	X	X	X	X	F	E	H	I	J
F. Swivel base	X	X	X	X	X	X	G	H	I	J
G. Color choice	X	X	X	X	X	X	X	H	G	J
H. Easy to clean	X	X	X	X	X	X	X	X	I	J
I. Quality reputation	X	X	X	X	X	X	X	X	X	J
J. Cost	X	X	X	X	X	X	X	X	X	X

Figure 2

Factor	# of times on Matrix	Rank
A. Sturdy	7	2
B. Folds to store	4	4
C. Comfort	9	1
D. Padded arms	4	4
E. Guarantee	1	9
F. Swivel base	2	8
G. Color choice	3	7
H. Easy to clean	4	4
I. Quality reputation	3	7
J. Cost	7	2

Figure 3

Option : Slouch Chair   Evaluation Form

Factors:	Acceptablity		Rank		Score
Sturdy	(1 2 3④5)	x	(2)	=	8
Folds to store	(1 2 3④5)	x	(4)	=	16
Padded	(1②3 4 5)	x	(4)	=	8
Guarantee	(1②3 4 5)	x	(1)	=	2
$35 price	(1 2 3 4⑤)	x	(2)	=	10

Option: Executive Swivel   Evaluation Form

Factors:	Acceptability		Rank		Score
Sturdy	(1 2③4 5)	x	(2)	=	6
Padded arms	(1 2 3④5)	x	(4)	=	16
Swivel	(1 2③4 5)	x	(2)	=	6
Guarantee	(1 2 3 4⑤)	x	(1)	=	5
$49 price	(1②3 4 5)	x	(2)	=	4

∼ Action Tip 25 ∼

Be ready to jump-start a stalled meeting.

A good decision-making strategy should help you keep the meeting moving along. However, even the best plans can occasionally stall. You can jump-start a stalled meeting by:

1. Restating the goal of the meeting.

2. Summarizing what has been accomplished so far. Don't assume that every member of the group knows exactly what is going on. A "time out" to recap what has been decided is sometimes necessary.

3. Ask everyone for a new approach. Let the group be jointly responsible for getting things moving again.

4. Table the discussion until later. Assign people to think about the roadblock and what might be done to overcome it.

Chapter 6

Concluding and Following Up Successfully

∼ **Action Tip 26** ∼

Record the group conclusion or decision.

Once a meeting is drawing to a close, check for consensus and be sure that the group's recommendations are correctly recorded. Word the conclusions clearly and accurately.

Acknowledge that some members may still disagree and let participants know that all concerns and objections have been noted—and will be expressed in the minutes. But don't let the objections of one or two derail the progress of the overall group.

Meeting notes should be recorded throughout the discussion. Good notes or minutes should provide a record of key points of the group's discussion, decisions, as well as follow-up activity. Make sure the task of minute-taking is assigned before the meeting begins, preferably to an individual who is likely to be an impartial observer—a departmental assistant, for example.

Circulate the minutes to all participants as soon as possible after the meeting and invite them to note corrections or additions as appropriate. Then keep the minutes on file in case future review becomes necessary.

～ Action Tip 27 ～

Assign specific follow-up actions.

Be sure that all meeting participants have their "marching orders." A brilliant decision will be of no value if it isn't implemented—and the people who made the decision are the best ones to direct implementation.

Follow-up assignments typically include informing people of the new action, training people in how to implement it, creating forms or written instructions for implementing it, and communicating to key people about the action and its timing. Before leaving the meeting, identify the tasks needed to implement the action and assign responsibility for each to a meeting participant.

Of course, there will undoubtedly be some required action from an individual or department not represented in the meeting. The task of notifying the appropriate individual must still be assigned to one of the meeting participants. Each action item, no matter how small or quickly dispensed with, should be assigned to a participant for follow-up.

∼ **Action Tip 28** ∼

Test for success.

We talked about evaluating ideas in Action Tip 22. In the midst of the discussion, such evaluation is based on our experiences and best guesses. This Action Tip addresses the "acid test"—based on actual results.

After an appropriate period of time, a follow-up meeting should be scheduled to evaluate the outcome of the decision. Did our idea work? De we really solve the problem? Did we achieve the results we wanted? Was the decision carried out the way we had anticipated?

Problems have ways of recurring in a cyclical pattern or reemerging in different variations. Seldom can a solution settle the matter once and for all. Action testing checks on implementation and should be readministered periodically.

If the solution didn't perform as hoped, it is time to look back and decide if it should be subjected to another meeting or if other administrative action should be taken.

～ Action Tip 29 ～

Make sure that assigned follow-up work is accomplished.

Don't let assigned follow-up actions slip through the cracks. Use meeting minutes to record who is to do what and note deadlines for each task. Then send reminder memos or calls before the input is required. Record each task on your calendar.

Take this responsibility as the meeting leader—don't be bashful about reminding people to follow through—or assign it to another meeting participant.

✎📁 **Chapter 7** ✎📁

Tracking and Developing Meeting Skills

～ Action Tip 30 ～

Track meeting evaluations over time.

Use a quick meeting evaluation form following each meeting. A sample form looks like the one on page 62—but feel free to modify this to get at factors you are concerned about.

In some cases, you may want to use average evaluation scores as shown here. Sometimes you may choose to track only one or two factors—especially meeting behaviors you are trying to improve. For example, if group conflict has been a problem, you may want to track this issue alone.

Sample meeting evaluation form

Listed below are seven statements relating to group competence. Please circle the number on the scales which best describes the performance of the group you have just participated in.

1. There was a high degree of involvement among participants.
   Strongly   Strongly
   Agree   5 4 3 2 1   Disagree

2. Commitment to group decisions by most members was:
   High   5 4 3 2 1   Low

3. Leadership (i.e., responsiblity for moving the group toward task accomplishment) moved from person to person as the meetng went on.
   Strongly   Strongly
   Agree   5 4 3 2 1   Disagree

4. Feelings were openly dealt with.
   Strongly   Strongly
   Agree   5 4 3 2 1   Disagree

5. A systematic approach was used to clarify the problem and establish criteria before solutions were considered.
   Strongly   Strongly
   Agree   5 4 3 2 1   Disagree

6. Confrontation and conflicting ideas were managed to improve the quality of the group's decision.
   Strongly   Strongly
   Agree   5 4 3 2 1   Disagree

7. The overall success of the group's perfomance should be evaluated as:
   High   5 4 3 2 1   Low

Total Score: _____

Several ways of tracking such information are shown on the following pages. Some people prefer to show changes over time, using a line graph (Figure 4) or a combination line graph with data chart (Figure 5). Word processing software can easily produce such charts and graphs.

Figure 4

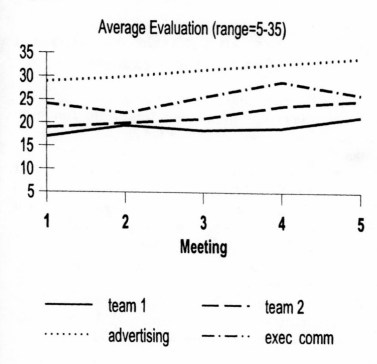

Average Evaluation (range=5-35)

| | team 1 | | | — — · | team 2 |
| | advertising | | | — · — ·· | exec comm |

Figure 5

(a data chart would be added to line graph)

team 1	16.98	19.4	18.44	19	21.4
team 2	18.9	19.95	21	23.7	24.9
advertisin	28.9	29.9	31.4	32.67	34
exec com	24.09	22.1	25.6	28.9	26.13

～ Action Tip 31 ～

Develop meeting skills among all organization members.

Despite the heavy use of meetings in most organizations, few people are adequately trained to run good meetings. Almost every organization would be wise to consider an investment in meeting management training to reduce the pitfalls and take advantage of the benefits of effective participative decision-making.

Ongoing evaluation and systematic improvement efforts make a lot of sense when you consider how much organizational time and effort go into meetings.

Don't forget the employees who may not spend a large portion of their time in meetings. Frequent and regular attendance of meetings will, of course, work to improve meeting preparation and management skills. But such skills are important for the infrequent users, as well.

This book, of course, provides a good start for anyone who may be called upon to attend a meeting. Occasionally, it may be useful to invite in a trainer or development specialist to monitor, analyze, and suggest improvements for your meetings. To do so, consult publications in human resource development and training for names of experts.

✏📁 **Chapter 8** ✏📁

The Behavioral Side of Successful Meetings[1]

The writings on running effective meetings focus on two major categories of suggestions for meeting leaders: recommendations for handling "nitty-gritty" meeting details and recommendations for managing interpersonal behavior.

The following checklist reviews key idea about both of these categories. It can serve as a quick reminder of many of the most important ideas in this brief book.

---

1. Some of this information is adapted from Steven H. Larson, "The Behavioral Side of Productive Meetings," transmitted on America On-Line, 1997. Larson is a communication analyst and instructor for Blue Cross of Northeast Ohio, Cleveland.

Meeting fundamentals

Be sure all participants know why they are there. This isn't am earth-shaking new principle, of course, but the importance of being absolutely certain all participants are aware of the meeting topic and of their expected role cannot be over-stressed. The tone of a good, productive meeting is set long before the actual meeting ever begins.

Start the meeting on time. While some people advise waiting for stragglers, I strongly recommend starting precisely on time. Waiting for latecomers becomes self-defeating. Starting on time tells participants that they are expected to be there and that you value their time. It is probably wise to schedule an initial activity for the first few minutes that will allow latecomers to catch up. If you give critical information at the very beginning, the few who may come late will be completely ineffective. So, push for promptness via setting an example of punctuality. But don't be such a stickler about it that latecomers will be out of it.

Keep your meetings on track. Encourage every participant's contribution in setting realistic goals for the group. When people participate in setting the goals, they are much more likely to buy-in. Once goals have been established, help participants stay on track and accomplish what they set out to do.

Be open to the suggestions and opinions of group members. Probably the greatest key to effective meetings is the establishment of an open and trusting atmosphere in which all members feel free to participate.

Encourage everyone to help control the meeting.
Point out when someone dominates the conversation. Encourage people to confront issues that upset them, but without heated, emotional arguments. When issues are bought up, participate and encourage participation in discussing them to everyone's satisfaction.

The dilemma in most problem-solving meetings that makes them so tricky to manage is that the subject of discussion is often an issue that arouses polarized and highly emotional opinions. Building your skills at managing interpersonal behavior, however, can help meetings operate smoothly.

The need for balanced participation

A crucial dimension of any meeting is the balance of participation among group members. Research verifies that as a group member's participation increases, so does his or her satisfaction with and commitment to the group. An old adage states that "people tend to support what they help create," to which we could add: "Nothing commits like commitment"—and the ultimate form of commitment is active participation.

Maintain a content vs. process focus. Don't mistakenly assume that the obvious content of a person's statement is all that needs to be addressed and that emotions can be ignored. Listen to what is said, but also try to interpret the feelings behind the statement. Nothing causes people to "clam up" faster than having their emotions ignored. Think about the last time someone ignored a statement you made about something that was important to you. How did you feel?

Be wary of the "freedom presumption." The freedom presumption assumes that because all people are "free" to participate, they will offer what they have to say. The reality is that many people feel inhibited about making their comments, even in the most open climate. Occasionally, meeting members need to be encouraged to share their thoughts. Silence should, at times, be tested. However, be aware that meetings where people feel forced to talk are as threatening as those where people feel afraid to do so.

Check your interpretation of member silence. When someone in the group remains silent, other group members sometimes use that person as a screen on which to project what they want the person to feel, e.g., agreement with their point of view. The message here is that silence isn't to be trusted until it has been checked out.

Beware of the leadership fallacy. Groups seldom have only one leader. Each participant can, and perhaps should, assert leadership. Effective leaders assume this. If one person must remain the only leader, much of the value of the group process is lost. When different people assume leadership at various points in the discussion, feelings of satisfaction, responsibility, and commitment increase, as does the perceived quality of the group's decisions.

Avoiding the perils of groupthink

When groupthink arises, members' statements begin to be policed by fellow members to ensure that no one upsets the apple cart by going against the group's way of thinking.

To avoid this, keep alert to the symptoms of this dysfunctional condition.

Red flags indicating possible groupthink

Lack of free expression. Dissenting viewpoints may be hindered by superior—subordinate relationships, collusion among subgroups, inappropriate leadership style or a judgmental group climate. The latter especially promotes defensiveness, and members become fearful of being evaluated and possibly embarrassed.

Self-censorship. Groupthink may be present when the group produces unanimous decisions that reinforce group uniformity. The more group members perceive themselves to think alike, the less likely they will be to deviate from "traditional" thinking.

Tunnel vision. Frequently after achieving cohesion, members start failing to examine carefully all the relevant options. They tend to lose insight and objectivity. Creativity drops sharply.

The process taboo. Some groups convey that it may be tabooed to talk about group process. Perhaps this taboo arises from a fear of looking "too closely lest one see too much," or perhaps people have fostered the idea that examining group behavior is a waste of time. No matter what the case, groups should develop the idea that looking at their process (interpersonal relationships, task management, decision making, etc.) is a healthy thing to do. Stopping periodically during the discussion to comment on process can be very helpful. This is not a time-waster. A little time spent examining the process along the way may prevent major problems when time is really critical.

Anxiety avoidance. People like to avoid anxiety, and examining roles, relationships, and other such factors is anxiety-producing. After all, how do you turn to your supervisor and say, "Every time I propose an idea, you either run it over or steal it, and that makes me angry"? Honesty is hard to handle because the risk of provoking hostility is so high. But it can help prevent groupthink.

Combating groupthink

Legitimize disagreement. Leaders and participants should promote an atmosphere in which members feel free to disagree. This can be done by setting up rules about openness. Give minority viewpoints careful consideration. Encourage members to play devil's advocate. Don't mistake silence for agreement.

Generates ideas instead of evaluating them. Hold back or avoid immediate evaluation of solution proposals. Encourage free input of ideas and suggestions. Help the group develop a problem focus before getting into a solution focus.

Think through an idea more than once. Make it a habit to review decisions after enough time has elapsed for them to cool off. Don't convey the impression that a tentative solution is a final solution until it has been revisited.

Appreciate the value of conflict

Discussion and decision making inevitably lead to conflict; it's a natural and useful part of the process and should be openly dealt with by the group. Conflict that is merely smoothed over always resurfaces, and in a number of different ways.

The key difficulty in conflict management is that group members have an easier time recognizing symptoms of conflict than they do its root causes Symptoms can usually be quickly eliminated, thus giving the group the illusion of having removed the stumbling block. Dealing with symptom feels good for the group because of this short-term payoff, but the long-range effects can be quite costly.

When groups fail to take adequate time over the roots of conflict, they leave themselves open for potentially severe consequences. Conflict that is ignored ("I don't feel any conflict!"), thwarted ("You people settle those issues some other time; we've got work to do here!"), or glossed over ("Harry and Sue used to disagree about everything, and now they almost agree on something. Let's get to the next issue.") can all result in the disagreement spiraling to higher levels.

On the other hand, the group that effectively deals with conflict:

- Values high levels of interaction.
- Tolerates—in fact, welcomes—conflict for the airing of differences.
- Takes a problem-solving approach to conflict.
- Collaborates, rather than avoids, compromises, or competes.
- Processes the feelings behind participants' statements, as well as their content.
- Does not proceed with the task until the conflict has been managed to a point where all parties are satisfied with the outcome.
- Realizes that groups characterized by moderately high levels of well-managed conflict exhibit greater creativity and find higher-quality solutions.

✐📁 Appendix 1 ✐📁

Your Questionnaire Results

....

The attitude scales on the questionnaire presented earlier in this book (Chapter 1) measure six concepts. An asterisk (*) indicates reverse scoring where "strongly agree" is a negative response, etc.

The *necessity* of meetings held is measured by these items:

6. Seem to be substitutes for more meaningful work.(*)

12. Are called only when necessary.

17. Are scheduled too frequently.(*)

The degree to which meetings move logically to *closure* is measured by:

5. Often fail to reach a sense of completion.(*)

11. Move through the discussion phases efficiently.

16. Follow an agenda rather than wandering to different topics.

The degree to which the meetings permit *receptivity* to ideas is measured by:

10. Permit group members to freely participate and share ideas openly.

15. Allow offbeat or unusual ideas to be given a fair hearing.

4. Seldom result in creative solutions or ideas.(*)

The degree to which participants *feel good* about their group problem solving is measured by:

3. Result in participants' feeling good about the group's decisions.

9. Promote a commitment toward the organization by involving members in decisions.

19. Cause participants to gain a feeling of organizational unity.

14. Deal with agenda items that are not relevant to all participants in the group.(*)

The *efficiency* of the group process is measured by these questions:

2. Take up more time than they are worth.(*)

8. Usually result in decisions that could be more quickly made by one person working alone.(*)

13. Begin and end on time.

20. Seem to eat up too much of my workday.(*)

The *quality* of decisions made by groups is measured by the following:

1. Result in high-quality decisions.

7. Produce better solutions than could be produced by one person working alone.(*)

18. Are often dominated by a few members.(*)

Ranking the six concepts

The six concepts identified in the beginning of this appendix (efficiency, necessity, closure, quality, feel-good, receptivity) were ranked by those responding to the survey. (1 being most often identified as being a problem.)

Rank	Dislikes	Mean score on a 5-point scale
1	efficiency	3.286
2	necessity	3.143
3	closure	3.117
4	quality	2.964
5	feel-good	2.766
6	receptive	2.664

Some interesting perceptions about meetings

Based on my nearly 30 years of studying people's attitudes toward meetings, I offer the following generalizations:

Top four things that people found *disturbing* about the meetings they attend on the job:

1. Meetings fail to begin and end on time.

2. Meetings take more time than they're worth.

3. Meetings often fail to reach a sense of completion.

4. Meetings are often dominated by a few.

These responses overwhelmingly show a frustration with the *lack of efficiency* of meetings.

෨ ෨ ෨ ෨

Top four things respondents *liked* about the meetings they attend on the job:

1. Meetings permit group members to freely participate and share ideas openly.

2. Meetings promote a commitment toward the organization by involving members in decisions.

3. Groups produce better solutions than could be produced by one person working alone.

4. Meetings cause participants to gain a feeling of organizational unity.

People especially value the way meeting participation can help them feel good about the organization.

ഗ ഗ ഗ ഗ

Some interesting perceptions:

Individual comments about meeting experiences can be categorized into three groups:

1. **Positive statements about meetings attended.** (Examples: "Meetings create and support synergy, without which no dramatic results are possible," or "Very necessary, usually run effectively.")

2. **Negative statements about meetings attended.** (Examples: "Always too long; never concise," or "Our meetings are very one-way. They involve the same topics at every meeting— a vicious circle of repetition and nothing accomplished.")

3. **Statements that reflect mixed views or offer observations on how meetings should be.** (Examples: "They should have 1) a reason; 2) a set agenda; and 3) a specific time," or "They are effective when well planned and fairly administered.")

The comments support the theory that meetings can provide people with satisfying experiences, especially when the meetings create a receptive atmosphere—where people can really express ideas, share information, and confront problems without feeling unduly constrained. Given such opportunities, people feel good about their organization so long as they are not subject to meeting overkill.

To improve the probability that people will profit from meetings, leaders must be sensitive to the most common frustrations felt—failure to move the meeting along efficiently and reach solutions via a systematic problem-solving approach. Managers should also be wary of the overuse of meetings.

 **Appendix 2**

Sample Forms

....

Sample decision grid

SIMPLE CONSENSUS PRIORITY MATRIX										
ISSUE:										
FACTORS:	A	B	C	D	E	F	G	H	I	J
A										
B										
C										
D										
E										
F										
G										
H										
I										
J										

Sample decision grid

Factor	# of Times on Matrix	Rank
A.		
B.		
C.		
D.		
E.		
F.		
G.		
H.		
I		
J.		

Sample decision grid

Option:			Evaluation Form	
Factors:	Accept- ability		Rank	Score
	(1 2 3 4 5)	x	( ) =	
	(1 2 3 4 5)	x	( ) =	
	(1 2 3 4 5)	x	( ) =	
	(1 2 3 4 5)	x	( ) =	
	(1 2 3 4 5)	x	( ) =	

Option:			Evaluation Form	
Factors:	Accept- ability		Rank	Score
	(1 2 3 4 5)	x	( ) =	
	(1 2 3 4 5)	x	( ) =	
	(1 2 3 4 5)	x	( ) =	
	(1 2 3 4 5)	x	( ) =	
	(1 2 3 4 5)	x	( ) =	

Sample meeting evaluation forms

Based upon your own feelings and observations, how would you rate this meeting on the following?

1. To what extent were objectives clearly stated?
Completely   Completely
Unclear 1   2   3   4   5   6   7   8   9 Clear

2. To what extent was the knowledge of participants utilized?
  Not
  at all 1   2   3   4   5   6   7   8   9 Completely

3. To what extent was decision making shared by participants?
Dominated   Completely
By one 1   2   3   4   5   6   7   8   9 Shared

4. To what extent did people trust and level with each other?
Not Open   Completely
At All 1   2   3   4   5   6   7   8   9 Open

5. To what extent were all participants actively involved in the meeting?
Not at   To A Very
All   1   2   3   4   5   6   7   8   9 Great Extent

6. To what extent did leadership style contribute to meeting effectiveness?
Not At   To A Very
All   1   2   3   4   5   6   7   8 9 Great Extent

Sample meeting evaluation forms

1. To what extent did this meeting meet its stated objectives?
   Not At All 1 2 3 4 5 6 7 8 9 Completely

2. To what extent did this meeting achieve your personal objectives?
   Not At All 1 2 3 4 5 6 7 8 9 Completely

3. Which aspects of the meeting were most helpful to you?
   A. _____
   B. _____
   C. _____

4. Which aspects were least helpful to you?
   A. _____
   B. _____
   C. _____

5. What action steps will you be taking as a result of this meeting?
   _____
   _____
   _____
   _____
   _____
   _____

6. Other comments? Please use other side if necessary.
   _____
   _____
   _____
   _____
   _____

Sample meeting evaluation forms

Circle the number that best describes how well your group works together

	Low						High	
Task Accomplishment	1	2	3	4	5	6	7	8
Use of Time	1	2	3	4	5	6	7	8
Use of People's Ideas	1	2	3	4	5	6	7	8
Conflict Resolution	1	2	3	4	5	6	7	8
Goal Clarity	1	2	3	4	5	6	7	8
Teamwork	1	2	3	4	5	6	7	8
Effective Listening	1	2	3	4	5	6	7	8
Leveling	1	2	3	4	5	6	7	8

What can be done to improve participants working together?

_____

_____

_____

_____

_____

_____

Sample meeting evaluation forms

1. Objectives of the meeting were:

   9 8 7 6 5 4 3 2 1
   Completely   Unclear
   Understood   Misunderstood

2. Time utilization was:

   9 8 7 6 5 4 3 2 1
   Effective   Not
                      Effective

3. Exchange of views was:

   9 8 7 6 5 4 3 2 1
   Open and   Not Open
   Candid   Cautious

4. Conflicting points of view were:

   9 8 7 6 5 4 3 2 1
   Fully   Not
   Resolved   Resolved

5. Teamwork during the meeting was:

   9 8 7 6 5 4 3 2 1
   Excellent   Poor

In any situation where performance was not up to desired standard, what can be done to improve it? Be specific.

_____

_____

_____

_____

_____

_____

Sample meeting effectiveness tracking chart

Evaluation (Average score)	Meeting Dates and topic (e.g., Jan 3, 1999 marketing)								
	Sample								
1. Degree of involvement	4.1								
2. Commitment to decision	4.0								
3. Leadership	3.3								
4. Feelings dealt with	2.2								
5. Systematic approach	4.1								
6. Conflict management	2.7								
7. OVERALL SUCCESS	3.8								
TOTAL SCORE:	24.2								

Epilogue

A Closing Thought

....

I have long had a love-hate relationship with meetings. I still find poorly run meetings to be incredibly frustrating. When the principles covered in this book, however, are applied effectively, I often experience a genuine sense of satisfaction when a complex problem is solved.

The most critical points of a meeting are the beginning and end. The opening moments can often set the climate and tenor for the discussion. The conclusion, especially the implementation phase, determine whether the participants' time was wisely used.

Review the ideas in this book often. Make them a part of your organizational life, and you will dramatically enhance your success in holding successful meetings.

About the Author

Dr. Paul R. Timm is best known for bringing powerful, practical ideas to thousands of people through his writing, teaching, video programs, and speaking. He has served as consultant and trainer to numerous corporations, associations, and government agencies, dealing with challenges and opportunities in customer service, human relations, personal effectiveness and communication.

Timm has almost 30 years of front-line experience in people management, motivation, and business skill-building. He has held leadership positions with Xerox Corporation, Martin Marietta, Bell South, and was president of a training firm, Prime Learning International. He has continued to research contemporary management challenges, having received research grants from JCPenney Corporation and others. He serves on the editorial advisory board for Dartnell Corporation and Parke-Davis Pharmaceutical's *Patient Service Initiative* publications. His consulting focuses on customer service and retention in retail, financial, and health care organizations.

An active author, Timm has written 31 books and dozens of articles. He also wrote and appears in six videotape training programs produced by JWA Video of Chicago.

He earned university degrees from the State University of New York at Buffalo (bachelor's degree), Ohio University (master's degree), and Florida State University (Ph.D.). Dr. Timm has taught at three major universities and currently serves as chair of the Organizational Leadership and Strategy Department at the Marriott School of Management, Brigham Young University.

Index

Winning Telephone Tips,
How to Hold Successful Meetings
and
How to Make Winning Presentations
by Dr. Paul R. Timm

Winning Telephone Tips,
How to Hold Successful Meetings
and
How to Make Winning Presentations

by Dr. Paul R. Timm

prove your telephone skills and increase your profits! You'll learn why it's important to your own telephone calls, how to avoid unnecessary call screening and how to make voice-mail more efficient with **Winning Telephone Tips.**

e meetings a valuable business tool or a waste of time? When should a meeting be held when should a meeting be avoided? Learn to make meetings work for you with **How to Successful Meetings.**

ke the mystery and fear out of making a speech or a presentation with **How to Make ning Presentations.** Learn to feel comfortable and in control when speaking before one)00 people.

ch training program comes with a videocassette, audiocassette and copy of the book for $99.95.

t call toll-free, 1-800-327-5110.
 may use MasterCard, Visa or American Express.

complete the order form below and mail to the address in the ded area.

✂ cut here ✂

WA/Video, 921 W. VanBuren St., Suite 220, Chicago, IL 60607

Send me _____ copy(ies) of *Winning Telephone Tips.* ($99.95)

Send me _____ copy(ies) of *How to Hold Successful Meetings.* ($99.95)

Send me _____ copy(ies) of *How to Make Winning Presentations.* ($99.95)

ne _____

lress _____

y _____ State _____ Zip _____

 Phone _____ Evening Phone _____

Enclosed is a check for $_____.   ❑ PO #_____
Please charge $_____ to my credit card.* ❑ Visa   ❑ MasterCard

redit card number)   (Exp. date)   (Signature)

Printed in the United States
49012LVS00002B/1-51

9 781564 143259